THE LIBRARY OF
AMERICAN
LIVES AND TIMES™

SAM HOUSTON

For Texas and the Union

Walter M. Woodward

The Rosen Publishing Group's
PowerPlus Books™

For Leanne, Anne, and Wilbourn:
My Inspiration

Published in 2003 by The Rosen Publishing Group, Inc.
29 East 21st Street, New York, NY 10010

First Edition

Editor's Note: All quotations have been reproduced as they appeared in the letters and diaries from which they were borrowed. No correction was made to the inconsistent spelling that was common in that time period.

Library of Congress Cataloging-in-Publication Data

Woodward, Walter M.
Sam Houston : for Texas and the Union / Walter M. Woodward.— 1st ed.
    p. cm. — (The library of American lives and times)
Includes bibliographical references (p.) and index.
ISBN 0-8239-5739-X (alk. paper : lib. bdg.)
1. Houston, Sam, 1793–1863—Juvenile literature. 2. Governors—Texas—Biography—Juvenile literature. 3. Legislators—United States—Biography—Juvenile literature. 4. United States. Congress. Senate—Biography—Juvenile literature. 5. Texas—History—To 1846—Juvenile literature. [1. Houston, Sam, 1793–1863. 2. Governors. 3. Legislators.] I. Title. II. Series.
F390.H84 W66 2003
976.4'04'092—dc21

                         2001006175

Manufactured in the United States of America

CONTENTS

Introduction

Some time in your life you have probably heard the name Sam Houston. His service to the United States and to Texas spanned almost fifty years. During the 1800s, he served as a soldier, a general, a U.S. congressman and senator, the president of a country, and a governor. He was the only person to serve as governor of two states, Tennessee and Texas. He was a citizen of five nations: the United States, the Cherokee, Mexico, the Republic of Texas, and the Confederate States of America.

As the United States expanded to the West, Sam Houston established himself as one of the most important and colorful figures to appear on the American frontier. When his honor was tested, Sam Houston risked his career, his reputation, and his life for Texas and for the Union. That commitment places Sam Houston alongside other great individuals who shaped not only the history of Texas, but also that of the United States.

Opposite: This picture of Sam Houston is from a daguerreotype made in 1859, while Houston was governor of Texas. Houston is best known for his role in Texas history, but he also worked extremely hard to preserve the Union and to prevent a civil war.

1. The Houstons of Timber Ridge

John Houston, his mother, his wife, and six of his seven children arrived in Philadelphia from Ireland in 1735. After a brief stay, they moved on to Lancaster County, Pennsylvania. The first years in Lancaster were successful, but the promise of cheaper lands south of Pennsylvania encouraged the Houstons to look for another place to settle.

In 1739, Benjamin Borden received a grant of 92,100 acres (37,272 ha) from William Gooch, royal governor of Virginia. The inexpensive land in Borden's grant in western Virginia offered the Houstons the possibility to improve their financial situation. Around 1842, they traveled the Great Wagon Road south through Maryland and down the Shenandoah Valley, settling in what is now Rockbridge County, near present-day Lexington, Virginia.

The Houstons prospered, but life on the frontier was always uncertain. In 1754, John Houston was killed in a farming accident. His oldest son, Robert, had been successful. He had purchased property at Timber Ridge and had become a leading citizen there. However, in 1761,

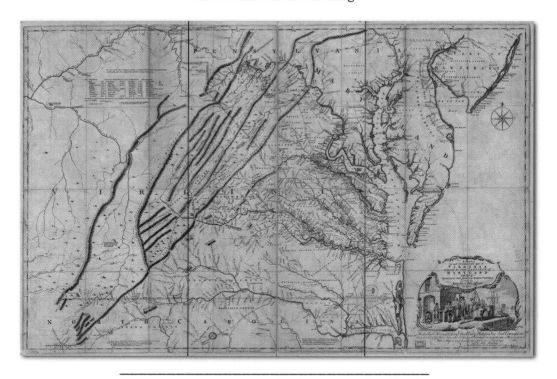

This hand-colored map shows the most inhabited part
of Virginia. It contains the whole province of Maryland with
parts of Pennsylvania, New Jersey, and North Carolina.
Drawn by Joshua Fry and Peter Jefferson in 1751, the map
was published by Thomas Jefferys of London in 1855.

Robert died unexpectedly, leaving the property at Timber
Ridge to John's youngest son, Samuel Houston, Sam
Houston's father, who was just a boy at the time.

During the time that the Houston family was going
through these difficulties, America was also having problems. Both England and France believed that they had
rights to the lands and natural resources in North
America. Generally the French controlled Canada and
lands around the Mississippi River, and Britain had
colonies from the East Coast of North America to the

Appalachian Mountains, but boundaries were fuzzy. Throughout the mid-1700s, colonists fought small battles to protect land that they believed was theirs. Finally, when France and England declared war on each other in Europe, these small battles in the colonies became an outright war, called the French and Indian War. From 1754 to 1763, British and American colonists fought against the French and their Indian allies. With the end of the war, the French were expelled, but Indian raids continued. Settlers on the frontier were left to protect themselves. Their feeling of independence only made them more determined to control their own future.

The French and Indian War had an important effect on the colonies. The British changed the way they governed their colonies in America. The war had been expensive, and to pay off debts, the British decided to make the colonists pay taxes. They also decided to leave British troops in the colonies, both to protect them from attacks by hostile Native American groups and to enforce treaties made with Native Americans that stated colonists would not settle past the Appalachians. The direct taxes and the presence of the British army only angered the colonists and increased resistance to British control.

Several events caused tensions to boil over, including the Stamp Act, the Boston Massacre, and the Tea Act. Finally, when British troops marched on Lexington and Concord on April 19, 1775, the first shots of the American Revolution were fired. The colonists officially declared

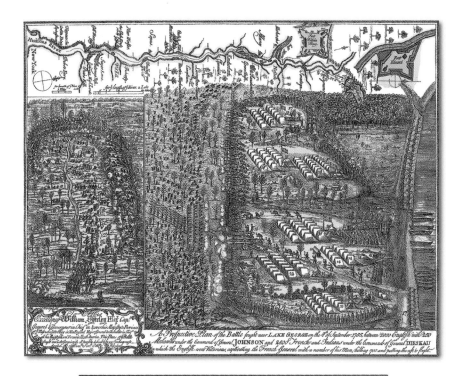

This 1768 map shows the Battle of Lake George on September 8, 1755, during the French and Indian War. The map shows the position of about 2,000 English soldiers, their 250 Mohawk allies, and the 2,500 French and Indians. This map was engraved by Thomas Jefferys and was published in London by R. Sayer as part of a general topographic map of North America and the West Indies.

their independence in Philadelphia on July 4, 1776. Samuel Houston joined the Continental army, determined to defend his rights. During the Revolution, he served in the Virginia Rifle Brigade under Daniel Morgan. They fought at the battles of Cowpens and Guilford Courthouse and were present for the British surrender at Saratoga. Samuel returned to Timber Ridge after the war to manage his farm. However, he enjoyed military life, so he continued to serve as an inspector of the Virginia militia and to work on the farm.

The handsome Captain Houston soon attracted the attention of Elizabeth Paxton, the daughter of another farmer. The couple married and settled in the fine, two-story home at Timber Ridge.

The Houstons had a happy marriage even though Samuel's military duties required his being away from home for long periods of time. During the first ten years of their marriage, the Houstons had four sons: Paxton, Robert, James, and John. On March 2, 1793, the Houstons celebrated the birth of their fifth son, and his father's namesake, Samuel, or Sam Houston, as he would come to prefer. After Sam, the Houstons had one son, William, and three daughters: Isabella, Mary, and Eliza.

Elizabeth Houston devoted her energy to the farm, her home, and her children. The boys attended the nearby academy, but only for a few months at a time. Elizabeth supervised much of the children's education at home.

As a young boy, Sam showed signs that he would do things his own way. Sam's older brothers began assigning him chores at age four, but he soon realized that farming was not for him. He found excuses to avoid work and wandered away from home to explore the countryside.

Sam's father had acquired a library that was considered sizeable for its day. Elizabeth encouraged reading as the first step in the children's education. As soon as Sam learned to read, he discovered that books offered as much of an escape as did the hills and the meadows. He could journey to faraway places and different times in history.

Sam also enjoyed hearing about the American Revolution and its heroes. George Washington, Thomas Jefferson, and James Madison were all Virginians. One of Sam's favorite places was the natural rock bridge located on land owned by Jefferson. In 1799, the black armband worn by his father at the death of George Washington made a lasting impression on Sam. He also heard exciting stories of the dangers that settlers experienced as they moved west from the Atlantic coast.

Captain Houston's military career was hard on the family's finances. As a militia inspector, he had to pay his own expenses. By 1806, the Houstons had decided to sell

In the 1700s and 1800s, many people decided to seek their fortunes on the western frontier. They often made their way west in wagon trains, as shown in this 1869 drawing by Henry Bryan Hall, entitled *Emigrants Crossing the Plains*.

the farm and to move to Tennessee. Some of the Houstons' relatives had moved to eastern Tennessee and had reported that they were doing well. Sam's father purchased land, and the family began preparing for the move. While on an inspection tour of military units, Captain Houston died suddenly. This occured in either 1806 or 1807, there is some debate about the exact date. The death of her husband did not stop the strong-willed Elizabeth Houston from carrying out the family's plans to make a new start in Tennessee.

2. The Raven

Elizabeth Houston settled her husband's estate, sold the Timber Ridge property, and paid the family's debts. This left the family with just enough money to begin a new life in Tennessee. She and her nine children loaded two wagons with only the necessary belongings and set out on the Wilderness Road. The Houstons traveled through the small villages of Knoxville and Maryville, Tennessee. They continued another 10 miles (16 km) to the 419 acres (169.5 ha) on Baker's Creek that Sam's father had purchased before his death.

Everyone in the family was expected to help make their new home a success. Sam's older brothers were determined that he share in the work. The Houstons cleared their land, built a small but comfortable cabin, and planted crops. Their hard work paid off, and they saved enough to invest in a small store in town. During

Following Page: This 1816 map of Tennessee, formerly part of North Carolina, is a detail from a map of North America compiled by John Melish and engraved by John Vallance and Henry Schenck Tanner. The Houstons settled at Baker's Creek, outlined in blue in the inset.

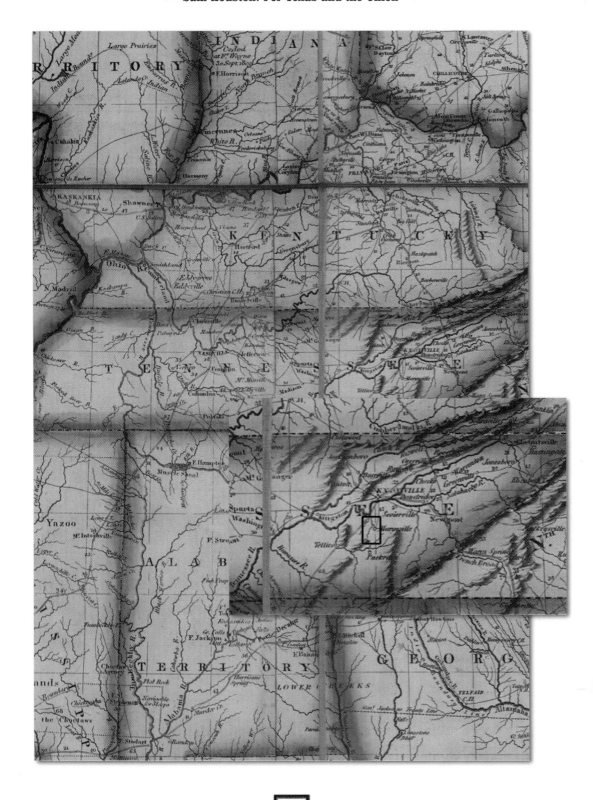

these first years, Sam's brothers Paxton and Robert and his sister Isabella died. This loss left his older brothers, James and John, in charge of the farm and the store. They also helped their mother raise the younger children.

Sam tried to do his share of the work, but he soon returned to his old ways. At age fourteen, he was handsome, popular, almost 6 feet (2 m) tall, and restless. He hated the dull routine of farming. He would disappear for hours into the woods around his home.

During Sam's wanderings, he often encountered Cherokee Indians who lived in eastern Tennessee and traded in Maryville. The great Cherokee Nation lay in the states of Tennessee, Georgia, Alabama, North Carolina, and South Carolina. Sam found the Cherokee friendly and peaceful.

Sam's brothers demanded that he continue his education. They enrolled him in Porter's Academy. Sam, at age sixteen, loved reading the Greek classics, especially Homer's *Iliad*. He also enjoyed reading about faraway places in geography books. However, he found the classroom too strict. Sam walked out, ending his formal education after less than a year.

Sam's brothers had another plan. They put him to work as a clerk in the family store in Maryville. Sam was miserable. One day in 1809, he disappeared.

After weeks with no word, the family heard that Sam had been seen with a group of Cherokee about 90 miles (145 km) away on Hiwassee Island, where the Hiwassee and Tennessee Rivers joined. James and John set out to find Sam, confident he would return with them. Settlers along the way directed them to the wigwam of Chief Oo-loo-te-ka, also known by his English name, John Jolly. They found Sam doing what he enjoyed most, reading. When they demanded he return home, Sam sprang to his feet and told them he preferred life with the Indians to the "tyranny" of his brothers. They returned home without their brother.

Sam wasted no time adopting the Cherokee ways and learning their customs. He wore their clothes and let his hair grow long. Sam soon learned the Cherokee language. Chief Oo-loo-te-ka understood that the death of Sam's father had left emptiness in the boy's life. Chief Oo-loo-te-ka filled that space by adopting Sam as his son. He taught Sam the importance of being honest and fair. Sam gained a respect for the Cherokee and for all Indians that continued for the rest of his life.

To prove Sam's acceptance to their group, the Cherokee gave him the name Colonneh, or the Raven. In Cherokee legend, the raven is honored for saving the Corn Spirit from an evil spirit, allowing the Cherokees' corn crops to grow.

For three years, Sam spent most of his time with the Cherokee, but occasionally he returned to Maryville. During these visits, the townsfolk were shocked by his looks and dress. Most people considered him hopeless and wondered if he would ever amount to anything.

Chief Oo-loo-te-ka, also known as John Jolly or Col-le, is shown here in George Catlin's 1834 painting. The chief was a mentor and father to Sam Houston. As more and more Cherokee were moved west in the 1800s, Oo-loo-te-ka urged them to join together and to become an independent nation. He wrote, "Instead of being remnants & scattered we should become the United Tribes of America . . . (and) preserve the sinking race of native Americans from extinction."

In 1812, Sam, at nineteen years old, decided the time had come to return home. He needed to live up to his responsibilities and to settle his debts. Much to everyone's surprise, he decided to open a school. Sam's enthusiasm persuaded families in the area to take advantage of this opportunity for education. Sam, dressed in a hunting shirt and wearing his hair in a braid down his back, held classes for eighteen students either in a one-room log building or outdoors on warm days. He found teaching a rewarding experience. Years later Sam recalled to an old friend that as a teacher, he "experienced a higher feeling of dignity and self-satisfaction than from any other office or honor which I have held."

3. "You Shall Hear of Me"

In 1812, the same year that Sam Houston opened his school, the United States declared war on Great Britain. Since the end of the American Revolution in 1783, the United States had been caught in the continuous struggle between the British and the French. The United States tried to remain neutral, but tensions increased as both nations captured American ships. Many Americans favored expanding the boundaries of the United States. They wanted the British out of Canada and the Spanish out of Florida. Those living on the frontier disliked the British and were fearful of their aiding the Indians against the United States. Finally, in June, the "War Hawks" in Washington got their wish and President James Madison signed a declaration of war.

Army recruiters, accompanied by the rousing music of a fife and a drum, arrived in Maryville early in 1813. They stopped in front of the courthouse and placed a number of silver dollars on the drum. Anyone wanting to enlist could step forward and collect his bounty. Houston, who happened to be passing, stepped out of the crowd and

As Sam Houston opened his school, the War of 1812 was beginning. This view of the famous Battle of Queenston Heights, which took place on October 5, 1812, was engraved by T. Sutherland. The engraving is based on a sketch by James Dennis, an officer who took part in the battle. It shows the American forces crossing the Niagara River from Lewiston, under fire from the Canadian militia and the British regulars.

removed a silver dollar. He enlisted as a private in the infantry. Sam was criticized for his decision. The son of an officer and veteran of the American Revolution had enlisted as a common soldier. Sam assured them, "You don't know me now, but you shall hear of me."

Elizabeth Houston understood her son's decision. She called Sam to her side and gave him a musket, saying "never disgrace it: for remember I had rather all my sons should fill one honorable grave, than one of them should

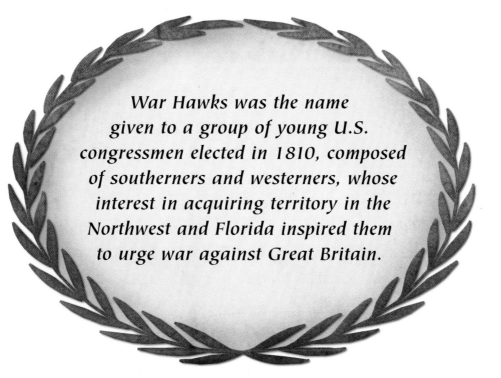

War Hawks was the name given to a group of young U.S. congressmen elected in 1810, composed of southerners and westerners, whose interest in acquiring territory in the Northwest and Florida inspired them to urge war against Great Britain.

turn his back to save his life." She told him to remember always, "While the door to my cottage is open to brave men, it is eternally shut against cowards." Elizabeth Houston placed a small gold band on his finger with a one-word inscription, HONOR.

Creek Indians in the southeast saw the War of 1812 as a chance to force white settlers from the land. The Creek, however, disagreed over whether to fight. About one thousand Creek, called Red Sticks because of their painted war clubs, vowed to wage war. In the summer of 1813, they attacked and burned American fort Mims, north of Mobile, Alabama, killing almost five hundred settlers.

The Tennessee governor asked Senator Andrew Jackson to take command of the militia and to put down the Creek uprising. After a series of battles, neither side could claim victory. The Creek retreated to a position on the Tallapoosa River named Tohopeka, or Horseshoe Bend. With the river protecting them on three sides, the Creek constructed a double log wall and earthen breastworks across the narrow neck to defend against an attack.

Sam Houston showed leadership qualities and in July 1813, he was promoted to the rank of ensign and was transferred to the Thirty-ninth Infantry Regiment. In December, he became a third lieutenant. Houston's regiment received orders to join Jackson's militia in Alabama.

Arriving on February 14, 1814, Houston took an active role in helping to train the militia for battle. For the next month the regulars, the militia, the friendly Creek, and the Cherokee readied themselves for an assault on the Creek fortress. In mid-March the entire group advanced to Fort Williams and then marched to Horseshoe Bend. Jackson's forces of about 3,000 men reached Horseshoe Bend on March 26.

The next morning, Jackson ordered an attack on the Creek fortress. Repeated attacks were turned back. Then a group of Cherokee crossed the river and returned with enough canoes to ferry back a force. When Jackson saw smoke coming from the fortress, he realized their attack was successful. With that force attacking from the rear, Jackson ordered a direct assault on the breastworks, pinning the Creeks between his two armies.

Houston's regiment led the charge. When Sam Houston reached the top of the breastworks, an arrow pierced his thigh, and he fell to the ground. Twice he tried to remove the arrow but failed. Finally, Houston forced a fellow soldier to rip the arrow from his leg. Sam Houston retreated, wounded and bleeding. Andrew Jackson witnessed the event. When Houston asked to rejoin his men, Jackson refused and ordered him from the battlefield.

The attack forced the Creeks to retreat to the river, but they were trapped in the logs and brush on the bank by rifle fire. When Jackson called for volunteers to force them out, the wounded Sam Houston grabbed his musket and led the charge. Within a few yards of the Creeks, two musket balls tore into his shoulder and upper arm. Houston called for his men to follow, but they did not, and he fell to the ground. The Creeks were finally forced out when troops set fire to the logs and the brush. General Jackson had a victory. The Red Sticks were defeated.

Houston's friends carried him back to the surgeon for treatment. The doctor removed one musket ball but left the other, thinking Houston could not possibly survive the night. The next morning the doctors thought Houston had little hope. He was placed on a stretcher and was carried back to Fort Williams. At Fort Williams, Houston recovered enough to begin the long journey home.

When Houston was pierced by an arrow at the Battle of Horseshoe Bend, he forced a soldier to pull the arrow from his leg so he could continue fighting, as shown in this engraving by B. Ross.

This is a silver service crafted by M. W. Galt and
Brothers from the $500 in silver coins Sam Houston received
as payment for his service in the War of 1812. It was common
for families with enough wealth to have some silver melted
down to create silverware or tea services such as this one.
This service is now held by the Sam Houston Memorial Museum.

Houston's courage and spirit at the Battle of
Horseshoe Bend caught Andrew Jackson's eye. He saw
something he liked in the young soldier.

Houston returned to Maryville so weak and frail that
his mother hardly recognized him. As news of his actions
at Horseshoe Bend spread in the community, Houston
knew he had fulfilled his promise to the people of
Maryville. They had heard of Sam Houston.

4. A Rising Star

In January 1815, news of Andrew Jackson's victory over the British at New Orleans, as well as the end of the war, arrived in Maryville. Houston hoped to stay in the army and in May, he was commissioned as a second lieutenant. In January 1817, Houston received orders to report to the southern district, in Nashville, commanded by Jackson. The southern district's offices were located at the Hermitage, Jackson's home. While there, Houston developed a close friendship with Jackson. In May, Houston was promoted to the rank of first lieutenant.

The Cherokee in eastern Tennessee had signed a treaty with the American government in 1817, giving up their homes in exchange for lands west of the Mississippi River. The War Department needed someone to administer the treaty. Sam Houston was qualified. He spoke the Cherokee language and knew many of the people who were being moved. Houston found himself torn between his duty and his concern for his Cherokee friends. He decided that the move was for the best, and that he would make it as easy as possible for them.

Andrew Jackson purchased the Hermitage, shown here in an 1818–1819 engraving, in 1804. In 1819, construction began on a federalist-style home of red brick. This building was destroyed in a fire, and Jackson rebuilt a fourteen-room home in the Greek Revival style, with six columns on the front.

In 1818, Houston accompanied a delegation of Cherokee chiefs to Washington. In March, the delegation, with Sam Houston dressed in Cherokee clothes, met with Secretary of War John C. Calhoun. While the Cherokee met with President James Monroe, Calhoun gave Houston a stern lecture on wearing Cherokee clothes while an officer in the U.S. Army. Houston said he only wanted to show respect for his delegation. Calhoun warned him not to make the same mistake again.

Two days later Calhoun again called Houston to his office. Someone had charged Houston with being

Houston is dressed in formal Cherokee clothing in this miniature portrait done around 1830. The portrait was copied from a painting done on silk at Brown's Indian Queen Hotel in Washington, D.C.

involved in illegal slave trade. The charges were proven false. He was insulted and angry. Houston never forgot the incident or his hatred of Calhoun. He resigned from the Army before he left Washington.

Houston returned to Tennessee confident he had done his best. He had already decided to move to Nashville and to study law in the office of Judge James Trimble. Normally an apprentice studied the law for at least a year and a half before taking the required exam. After only six months, Houston took the exam, passed it, and received his law license. He established a law practice in Lebanon, Tennessee, but in 1819, after less than a year, Houston left his practice to fill the office of attorney general of the Nashville district, to which he had been elected. The position did not pay enough, so he soon resigned and returned to his law practice.

Houston's popularity grew. In February 1823, he announced himself as a candidate for U.S. Congress. As Jackson's handpicked candidate, he received every vote.

Sam Houston set out for Washington with a letter of introduction from Andrew Jackson to Thomas Jefferson, the retired elder statesman of the Democratic Party.

After a brief visit with Jefferson at Monticello, he continued his trip to the nation's capital. He served two terms in the U.S. Congress and carried out his duties with care and concern, working hard to learn the operations of government and to develop his skills as a politician.

In the presidential election of 1824, Andrew Jackson received the greatest number of electoral votes. However, it was not a majority over John Quincy Adams, William Crawford, and

Major General Andrew Jackson, shown here at the Battle of New Orleans in an 1856 color lithograph by Charles Severin, was also known as Long Knife and Old Hickory. This lithograph was printed by Boell and Michelin in New York.

Henry Clay. Crawford suffered a stroke, which took him out of the running. With no majority, the decision went to the House of Representatives, as required by the U.S. Constitution. Henry Clay threw his support in the House of Representatives to John Quincy Adams, guaranteeing Adams a victory. Henry Clay then accepted an appointment as secretary of state in Adams's administration. Sam Houston and other supporters of Andrew Jackson

W.A. BLOUNT

William Blount is shown here in a painting by
Jacob Marling, a painter from North Carolina. Blount
lived from 1767 to 1835. He was prominent in politics
in Tennessee. This portrait may date from the late 1790s.

promised to overturn what they called the Corrupt Bargain in the next election.

After two terms in Congress, Houston decided to run for governor of Tennessee. Among Jackson's choices as candidates were James K. Polk, John Bell, and Sam Houston. Jackson picked Houston to run against Willie Blount and Newton Cannon, both of whom opposed Jackson's policies. Houston campaigned across the state, using his likable personality and persuasive speaking skills to appeal to voters. He won by more than eleven thousand votes. On October 1, 1827, at the First Baptist Church in Nashville, Sam Houston took the oath as governor.

Houston continued the policies of the previous administration. He also encouraged government support of trade, government relief for settlers struggling to pay for their land, and government funding for public education. He believed a state had a right and a responsibility to manage its own affairs, rather than to have to depend on the federal government.

In 1828, Jackson ran for a second time for president in one of the dirtiest presidential campaigns in U.S. history. Personal attacks on Jackson's character and marriage were especially hard on his wife, Rachel. Houston and other Jackson supporters celebrated when the totals were counted and Jackson had defeated Adams. The celebration turned to sorrow when Jackson's beloved Rachel died of a heart attack two days before Christmas. Jackson blamed Rachel's death on the cruel personal attacks that had occured during the campaign. He left for Washington, D.C., vowing never to forget what his enemies had done.

Houston returned to his duties as governor. At age thirty-five, he thought it was the time to consider his future and possibly marriage. His looks, colorful dress, and likable qualities appealed to women, but no serious romantic attachments had developed.

As governor, he would have been considered an ideal husband for any woman. It was Eliza Allen, a beautiful young woman from a wealthy family in Gallatin, Tennessee, who captured Houston's heart. After a brief courtship, Houston asked Eliza's father, John Allen, for permission to marry her. Allen approved of the match. Eliza Allen agreed. On January 22, 1829, Houston and Eliza married. The Houstons left the next day for Nashville and made their home at the Nashville Inn.

Houston decided to run for reelection as governor. He kept busy with his official duties and campaigning. On April 9, after less than three months of marriage, he returned home and found that Eliza had left him. Although we might never know the reasons for the separation, it is clear from a letter Houston wrote to John Allen that Eliza was unhappy.

Houston was devastated. He locked himself in his room as rumors about the reason for their separation spread throughout Nashville. Houston would not see anyone but his closest friends, who begged him to answer the rumors and charges. In a final attempt to get Eliza back, he went to the Allens' home and pleaded with her to forgive him. She refused. Houston returned to his room at the Nashville Inn. The next day, in a letter, he assumed the blame for the whole situation and resigned as governor of Tennessee. Sam Houston told his friends it was better he suffer the consequences alone. Houston would not answer any of the rumors, saying it was "a painful but private affair. I do not recognize the right of the people to interfere."

Many years later and 1,000 miles (1609 km) away, a friend asked Houston why the marriage had failed. He assured Houston that history would want to know. Houston asked him if he could keep a secret. The man eagerly answered, "Of course I can." Sam Houston's answer was simple, "Well so can I."

The reason for Houston and Eliza's separation will never be known. This was the lowest point in Houston's life. He sank into depression and despair. He turned to alcohol hoping it would ease his pain. This could have been the last anyone heard of Sam Houston, but it was not. Instead this dismal experience changed his life.

On April 23, 1829, Sam Houston left Nashville with his political career in ruins. He had no money, and his future was unsure. As he had done when he was a boy, he escaped to the only sanctuary he knew, the Cherokee and Chief Oo-loo-te-ka.

5. "My Wigwam Is Yours"

As Sam Houston made his way to the Cherokee Nation, he wrote Andrew Jackson describing himself as "the most unhappy man now living." When he finally arrived, Chief Oo-loo-te-ka welcomed Houston, telling him, "My wigwam is yours. Come rest with us." On October 21, 1829, Houston became a citizen of the Cherokee Nation.

This was a troubled time for the Cherokee, and Sam wanted to help. The Cherokee had first settled in Arkansas but were forced to move again to the Indian Territory, in present-day Oklahoma, under a treaty in 1828. They were promised $50,000 in gold for leaving their lands in Arkansas. Instead, they had received payment in certificates, which proved worthless. They also wanted good titles to their new lands. The Cherokee were concerned that other Cherokee groups from the East would be moved to their area with no provision for additional land. Also, the agents assigned to deal with the Indians were often corrupt. Several agents were profiting at the expense of the Indians and needed to be removed. In December, Houston, as an

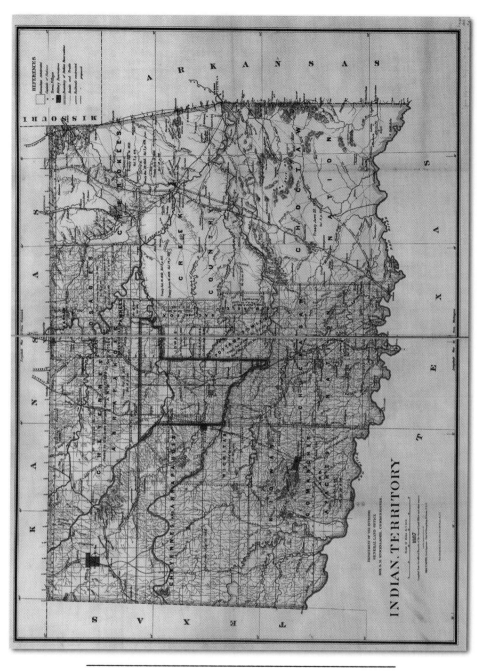

As Americans continued to settle in the West, the Native Americans
were pushed out. The Indian Territory, today's Oklahoma, was
land that was set aside for transplanting, or moving, Indian tribes
that were "in the way" of westward expansion. This 1887 map
was compiled from the official records of the General Land Office
and other sources under the supervision of George U. Mayo.

For the *Arkansas Gazette.*

THE INDIANS!—CHAPTER FIRST.

...ries, and ...censure. They ... is a point of endurance ... lic trust, and therefore deserve public demand... tion! And however earnest the writer of this article may be, in his wishes to see all the Indians, now residing East of the Mississippi, removed to Arkansas, he must confess, that, until the Government does appoint honest and capable Agents, for the different tribes already here, it would be a hapless journey for those to undertake who are in search of peace or happiness. Were it not for the injustice of the Agents to the Indians, on the Arkansas, I should deem it the most appropriate abode of the Indian. He might indeed look to this, as a land of happiness and contentment. But until suitable Agents are sent to them, they can only regard this as the land of *promises!* where fraud will supplant faith, and injustice triumph over humanity! At this very moment many emigrants are destitute of provisions promised to them by Government, under the treaty of 1828, while hundreds are ready to furnish the accustomed rations at six or seven cents each.— When will justice be done? *Delenda est Carthago!* TAH-LOHN-TUS-KY.

SUNDAY MAILS.

The following communication, from the Rev. Mr. HENRY, a young, but highly respectable and promising member of the Methodist Church, is published in pursuance of a rule

One of Sam Houston's articles, signed TAH-LOHN-TUS-KY, published in the June 22, 1830, issue of the *Little Rock Gazette,* is outlined in red here. In it he writes Indians "might indeed look to this, as a land of happiness and contentment. But until suitable Agents are sent to them, they can only regard this as the land of *promises;* where fraud will supplant faith, and injustice triumph over humanity!"

ambassador appointed by Chief Oo-loo-te-ka, and a delegation representing other Cherokee groups went to Washington, D.C., to ask for help.

In Washington, D.C., Houston was pleased to see his old friend Andrew Jackson and was thankful that their friendship was intact despite his troubles. Jackson ordered surveys to establish good titles to Cherokee land, and he removed several corrupt Indian agents. Before returning home, Houston and a New York investor submitted bids for supplying rations to Indians moving west.

Houston returned to the Indian Territory, in present-day Oklahoma, during the spring of 1830. He built a log house and established a small trading post called Wigwam Neosho. He married Tiana Rogers, the beautiful daughter of a white trader and his part-Cherokee wife, in a Cherokee ceremony. Tiana was a widow whose husband had moved west with the Cherokee but had been killed in a battle with the Osage Indians. The fact that Houston technically was still married to Eliza did not matter to the Cherokee. That summer, he wrote a series of newspaper articles defending the Indians against dishonest agents. These agents had promised the Indians payment in coin but instead paid them in paper money, which had little value. They also cheated the Indians with short rations. In between articles, Houston also sank into periods of drunkenness and depression.

The next spring, in 1831, Houston campaigned unsuccessfully for a seat on the Cherokee tribal council. His drinking and violent temper probably cost him the election. He once lost control and attacked Chief Oo-loo-te-ka.

Houston, still drinking and depressed, made a pointless trip back to Nashville, Tennessee, that summer. Almost at the moment of his return to Wigwam Neosho, he heard that his mother was very ill. He hurried back to Maryville, Tennessee, and remained by his mother's side until her death in September. Houston returned to Wigwam Neosho, wanting to make a change in his life. He had to stop drinking and to find a new path.

In December, Houston, acting only as a consultant, traveled with a Cherokee delegation to Washington, D.C., to try to get the government to honor its treaty obligations. He also had been contacted about a business arrangement that might provide a new opportunity.

The delegation arrived in Washington in late January 1830. Houston was not really needed, and he left for New York. A friend introduced him to a partner in the Galveston Bay and Texas Land Company. The company wanted Houston's help, as an attorney, to secure an old grant of land in Texas, then part of Mexico. No agreement was reached. He was back in Washington by April 1, 1832.

On April 2, a Washington newspaper reported on a debate in the House of Representatives. Congressman William Stanbery of Ohio asked whether Jackson's secretary of war, John Eaton, had been removed from office for illegally trying to award contracts for Indian rations to Sam Houston. When Houston read the article, his anger exploded. The next day he asked a friend to deliver a note to Stanbery, asking whether the quotes were correct. Stanbery refused to accept the note. For ten days, Houston waited for a reply. On April 13, Houston and some friends were walking on Pennsylvania Avenue when one of the men recognized Stanbery. Houston confronted him, and after the men exchanged words, Houston hit Stanbery over the head with a cane. After a struggle, Stanbery pulled a pistol from his pocket, but it misfired. Houston beat Stanbery until he lay motionless.

The next day, while still recovering, Stanbery sent a note to the Speaker of the House, demanding action. The rules of the House established that congressmen were protected from legal action against them for statements made while in session. The House voted to charge Houston for the attack and set a trial date.

The day of the trial, Houston's attorney, Francis Scott Key, only made a few brief remarks. Then Houston rose to defend himself. He claimed his right to question Stanbery's remarks because they were published in a newspaper, which was not exempt as was the floor of the House. Consequently, Houston maintained that the charges must be dropped.

The House debated for four days. Finally, they voted to convict Houston of "contempt in violation of the privileges of this house." On May 14, Houston again appeared in the House and received a formal reprimand, but no punishment. A jury found him guilty of

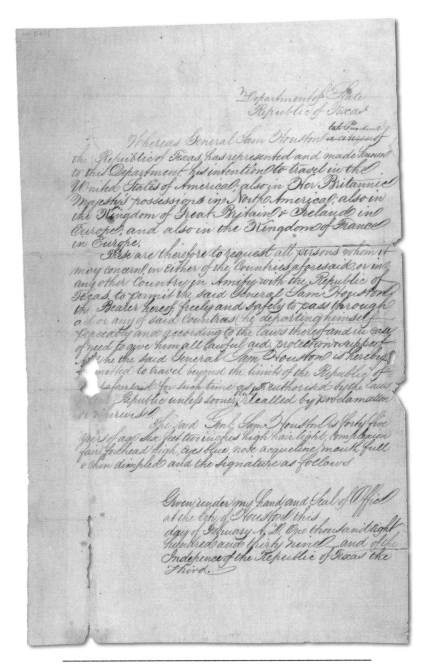

This is Sam Houston's passport, which was issued by the Republic of Texas in 1839. It allowed him to travel outside Texas. Above he is described as "Six feet two inches high hair light, complexion fair forehead high, Eyes blue, nose acqueline, mouth full & chin dimpled." Though this passport was issued when he was 45, the description is similar to that of his U.S. passport, which was issued when he was 38.

assault and fined him $500. Finally, a committee organized by Stanbery cleared Houston of the fraud charges.

Sam Houston had returned to the national spotlight. He explained, "They gave me a national tribunal for a theater, and that set me up again." No one was more pleased than Andrew Jackson. He had a mission for Houston. He wanted Houston to meet with the Comanche Indians in Texas. He needed an agreement that they would not fight other Indian nations the government moved west. Houston eagerly accepted Jackson's offer.

Houston reached Wigwam Neosho in early October and prepared to leave for Texas. Tiana would stay behind with the title to the land, their home, and their other property. Their marriage ended on good terms. Houston said his good-byes and headed south.

Sam Houston's passport stated that he was a citizen of the United States, thirty-eight years of age, six-feet-two-inches (188 cm) in height, with light brown hair and a light complexion. The passport requested that all tribes allow him to pass "safely and freely" through their territories. On December 2, 1832, he crossed the Red River into Texas.

6. "The Finest Portion of the Globe"

In 1821, Mexico gained its independence from Spain. The Mexican government viewed the colonization of Texas as a way to develop and to maintain control of its northern frontier. Moses Austin from Missouri received a grant of land to settle three hundred families from the United States in Texas. When he died unexpectedly, his son Stephen F. Austin continued the project. By the end of 1821, settlers began arriving on the lower Brazos and Colorado Rivers. Three years later, under the Mexican Constitution of 1824, favorable colonization laws increased the flow of Americans to the area even more.

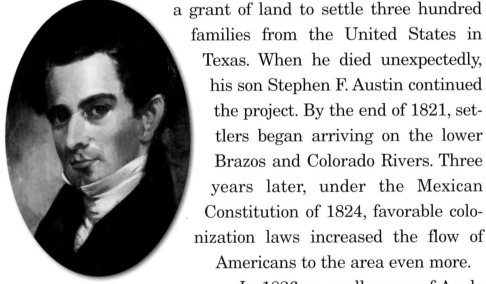

Stephen F. Austin is about 30 in this portrait, probably painted in Mexico City around 1820.

In 1826, a small group of Anglo citizens in Nacogdoches, Texas, declared their independence. This small rebellion ended quickly, but it raised concerns that Anglos and possibly the United States intended to acquire Texas. By 1830, thousands of Americans had moved to Texas to take advantage of cheap lands and to start new lives.

Following an inspection tour of Texas, the Mexican congress passed a new law on April 6, 1830, to maintain control. Concerned about the growing number of Americans in Texas, this law halted emigration from the United States and taxed imports and exports.

The arrival of troops and tax collectors alarmed Texans. They confronted the Mexican officials and forced them to leave Texas. Fifty-eight representatives from across Texas met in October 1832, to discuss the situation. They passed resolutions calling for an end to the emigration restrictions and the taxes for three years. They also called for a school system and for Texas to be an independent Mexican state. They agreed to meet again in April 1833.

In 1832, Sam Houston stopped in Nacogdoches on his way to San Antonio. Houston's reputation had preceded him and he agreed to stand for election as a delegate to April's meeting. He was in San Felipe by December 24. He applied for a land grant of 4,428 acres (1,792 ha).

Houston continued his journey to San Antonio where he met with the Comanche. He got their promise to meet with U.S. representatives at Fort Gibson in May 1833.

Houston returned to San Felipe, where he received his grant from Stephen F. Austin. He went back by the same route to Nacogdoches and then traveled to Louisiana.

At Natchitoches, Louisiana, Houston reported to the commissioner on his successful meeting with the Comanche and about the scheduled meeting in May. Houston also wrote to President Andrew Jackson, explaining the situation in Texas. He estimated that nineteen of twenty people would support the United States's acquiring Texas. Houston thought it "probable that I may make Texas my abiding place," but wrote, " I will never forget the country of my birth." Houston wrote to his cousin, "Texas is the finest portion of the Globe that has ever blessed my vision!"

Houston may have returned to Nacogdoches to campaign for election as a representative. On March 1, he was elected to attend the convention at San Felipe. At the convention, a majority of delegates did not support independence from Mexico. They hoped for a peaceful solution to their demands. The convention decided to restate their previous requests and to draft a constitution. Stephen F. Austin left for Mexico City to deliver the documents.

Austin arrived in Mexico City in July 1833, but political confusion delayed the government's answer. Discouraged, Austin wrote to friends in San Antonio suggesting they begin making plans to organize a separate state. He finally received the news that reforms would be implemented, but on the way home, he was arrested. Authorities had intercepted Austin's letter and thought he had suggested a revolt. He was held in Mexico City, without being charged, until the summer of 1835.

Meanwhile Houston settled in Nacogdoches, joined the Catholic Church as required by Mexican law, and opened a law practice. In November 1833, Houston petitioned for a divorce from Eliza Houston, but no action was taken until 1837.

During the years 1834 and 1835, most Texans, including Houston, were satisfied with the Mexican government's reforms. Texans were especially pleased with the repeal of the anticolonization law. Texans were still concerned because the Mexican government did not approve separate statehood, and Stephen F. Austin was still in prison. Houston knew trouble was brewing.

Mexican president Antonio López de Santa Anna pretended that he would allow the people more control over the government. Santa Anna soon reversed his position, however, and seized full power. President Antonio López de Santa Anna eliminated state governments

This portrait of General Antonio López de Santa Anna is believed to be from life, but the artist and date are unknown today.

and established military districts in the Mexican states south of the Rio Grande. He then set his sights on Texas.

Santa Anna again established customhouses and forts in Texas. In June 1835, Texans at Anahuac, led by William Barret Travis, forced Mexican troops to surrender. Texans now divided into the Peace Party and the War Party. The War Party called for a consultation to be held in mid-October to discuss the situation.

Austin returned from Mexico in September 1835 and encouraged Texans to defend their rights. News came that General Cos, Santa Anna's brother-in-law, was sending a large force to Texas. Houston knew that Texas needed to be prepared. He supported the meeting in October.

Mexican troops tried to recover a small cannon at Gonzales. On October 2, Texans in Gonzales raised a flag with a picture of a cannon and the words "Come and Take It." They fired the first shots of the Texas Revolution and won the battle against the Mexicans at Gonzales.

The military victory at Gonzales delayed the start of the Consultation. General Cos and his troops soon arrived in San Antonio, the only location in Texas that was controlled by Mexico.

Houston, a delegate to the Consultation, left Nacogdoches for San Felipe. When he arrived in late October, he learned that many of the other delegates were

---

Opposite: This 1837 map of Texas, based on one drawn by Stephen Austin, outlines each land grant plus an open area, in gray, for future grants. The bottom left lists a total of 14,050 families, of which 11,300 were on Austin's land.

This is a re-creation of the Come and Take It flag. The original disappeared. Some consider it to be the first Lone Star flag because of the single star above the cannon. When Texas declared its independence, it adopted a flag with a single star on it.

with Austin's army near San Antonio. Houston kept riding. He needed to bring back enough delegates to form a quorum. When he arrived in San Antonio, he urged the troops there to wait until a government could be formed before attacking. He recommended that they use the time to train. Austin agreed. The army voted that the delegates should leave immediately for the Consultation.

The Consultation met on November 1, at San Felipe. Houston knew that the delegates felt differently about how to react to the Mexican government's actions. Houston said it was important that the delegates agree on any decisions they made. They would be more effective this way. The Consultation followed the advice of the moderate group and decided not to declare Texas's independence from Mexico. They formed a provisional government for Texas as an independent Mexican state. The representatives called for another convention on March 1, 1836. On November 12, they chose Sam Houston to be major general and the commander of the armies of Texas.

In early December, Texan volunteers attacked San Antonio. After five days of fighting, General Cos surrendered and returned to Mexico. A few hundred Texans remained and converted the old mission, the Alamo, into a fort. Most volunteers left for home.

Houston knew that Texas still needed a trained army. The government, however, did little to support him. At the time, no one realized that Santa Anna, determined to put an end to the troubles in Texas, was preparing an invasion.

At Goliad, Houston got the news that part of Santa Anna's army had crossed the Rio Grande. Houston sent word to San Antonio that the men should blow

This portrait of General Cos, possibly styled after a painting done by William H. Croome around 1848, appears in John Frost's 1869 *Pictorial History of Mexico and the Mexican War.*

Alamo.

Bejar.

Campo Santo.

Mission de la Concepción.

Escala de 200. varas Castellanas.

Marzo de 1836.

up the Alamo and retreat to Gonzales, but he left the decision to the commander, James Neill. The men at the Alamo decided to stay to defend the main road into Texas.

Houston realized the situation looked bad. The Mexican army was preparing to invade Texas. In December 1835, Houston had predicted it would require 5,000 troops to defend Texas. In late January 1836, there was still no army. Houston left for Nacogdoches.

Houston spent the winter in Nacogdoches. In February, based on reports that the Cherokee might aid the Mexicans, Houston met with Chief Bowl, the leader of the Cherokee in Texas. Houston and Bowl signed Texas's first Indian treaty. Houston agreed to honor the Cherokee rights and lands if they stayed out of the conflict.

At the end of February 1836, Sam Houston arrived in Washington, Texas, with "more sensation than any other man." On February 27, the news came that Santa Anna's army had arrived in San Antonio. They had the Alamo and its defenders, including Jim Bowie, William Barret Travis, and Davy Crockett, under siege.

On March 1, the Texan delegates to the convention met at Washington. The next day, which was Houston's forty-third birthday, they adopted a declaration of

Previous spread: The 1836 map of the San Antonio-Alamo area was prepared by a Mexican army engineer for one of Santa Anna's generals. The map provided Santa Anna's soldiers with a view of the battlefield's hills, valleys, rivers, and other features. The Alamo pictured in the inset is an 1847 watercolor by Edward Everett. The Alamo was originally named San Antonio de Valero Mission.

In this cartoon, Houston has defeated Santa Anna and Cos. Houston is pictured saying, "You are two bloody villains, and to treat you as you deserve, I ought to leave you shot as an example! Remember the Alamo and Fannin!" Santa Anna replies, "I consent to remain your prisoner, most excellent sir!! Me no Alamo!!" Cos: "So do I most valiant Americano!! Me no Alamo!!"

independence. Two days later Houston was made commander of all the armies of Texas. On March 6, 1836, Houston left for Gonzales to organize an army and to relieve the Alamo. On March 17, the convention completed writing a constitution and setting up an interim government.

The newly formed Texan army, including those soldiers at the Alamo, Gonzales, and Goliad, totaled less than one thousand men. Houston wrote to James

Fannin, telling Fannin to abandon Goliad. On March 11, Houston arrived at Gonzales and found about 370 volunteers. Two Mexicans soon arrived with news of the Alamo. On the morning of March 6, 1836, after a thirteen-day siege, Santa Anna's army stormed the Alamo, massacred everyone, and burned the bodies. Houston realized the news "stirred up a feeling" in Texans "that was never to sleep again."

Houston faced a Mexican army of possibly five thousand trained soldiers. He had no choice but to retreat and buy time to recruit and train his men. He hoped his "Call to arms" would bring volunteers as they moved east.

As the Texan army retreated, so did thousands of settlers. Desperate to stay ahead of the Mexicans, Texans began what they called the Runaway Scrape.

When Fannin and his troops finally left Goliad, the waiting Mexican army captured them. The Texans were marched back to the fort. On March 27, Palm Sunday, the Texans were divided into three groups, were marched out of the fort in different directions, and were executed. Those remaining at the fort, including Fannin and the wounded, were also killed. Their bodies were burned.

Some in Houston's army wanted to fight. Houston later explained, "I held no councils of war. If I err, the blame is mine." At the end of March, the army had reached the Brazos River. They camped for ten days, using the time to reorganize, drill, and rest.

A Mexican army of about one thousand men reached the Brazos, south of Houston's position. The Mexicans could turn north and attack the Texans or cross the river and follow the government, which had retreated to Harrisburg, near the present-day city of Houston. The Mexicans, confident they could defeat Houston later, decided to pursue the officials. The government again retreated to New Washington on Galveston Bay.

Houston and his army decided to follow the Mexicans. When they reached Buffalo Bayou opposite Harrisburg on April 19, Houston discovered that the Mexican army had burned the town. Scouts crossed the bayou and returned with information that Santa Anna was commanding the troops headed for New Washington.

Houston seized the opportunity to trap Santa Anna. He crossed Buffalo Bayou and marched to Lynch's Ferry on the San Jacinto River. Houston wanted to cut off Santa Anna at New Washington. Houston's army camped in the trees lining Buffalo Bayou. The Mexicans had to cross the open prairie to reach the ferry. On April 20, 1836, as the Mexicans approached, they fired on the Texans. The Texans returned cannon fire and the Mexicans retreated and made camp.

On the morning of April 21, the Texans were restless. At midmorning General Cos arrived with more than five hundred soldiers to reinforce Santa Anna. The Mexicans numbered about 1,350 to Houston's 800 Texans. At noon, Sam Houston finally called a council of war. Houston,

however, had already made up his mind. The time was right to attack.

Houston ordered Vince's Bridge destroyed to prevent any retreat. At 3:00 P.M., Houston ordered his army into line across the plain of San Jacinto. The Texans knew the Mexicans were enjoying a siesta. To the cries of "Remember the Alamo! Remember Goliad!" the Texas army advanced with Sam Houston in front. The Mexican sentries opened fire when they realized what was happening. Houston's horse was hit by cannon fire and it fell to the ground. Houston mounted a riderless horse, but it too was struck. As the horse went down a musket ball shattered Houston's left ankle. He mounted a third horse, and with his boot filled with blood, he continued to lead the charge. The Texans quickly overwhelmed the Mexicans and the battle was over in just eighteen minutes. Finally, with the opportunity for revenge after Santa Anna's cruelty at the Alamo and at Goliad, the Texans' anger erupted and the killing continued into the night. The Texans killed 630 Mexicans and captured more than seven hundred. The Texans suffered two dead and thirty-four wounded, of which seven died later.

The next afternoon a scouting party captured a Mexican soldier dressed as a private. However, when the

Previous spread: Santa Anna is brought before Sam Houston after San Jacinto as Deaf Smith and other Texans look on in this 1886 re-creation by William Huddle entitled _Surrender of Santa Anna_. Houston, who is lying down because of his wounds, offers the defeated general a seat on an ammunition box before accepting his surrender.

Mexican prisoners shouted "El Presidente," Sam Houston knew that Santa Anna was a prisoner of the Texan army. The war for Texas independence was finished.

Houston remained at San Jacinto until government officials came to take charge of Santa Anna and to conduct peace negotiations. Houston's wound had become so serious that he could not delay treatment any longer. He said good-bye to the troops and sailed to Galveston, where he boarded the small trading ship, *Flora*, which was bound for New Orleans.

Houston wrote a letter to to his wife in 1853, in which he mentions the wound he received at San Jacinto in 1836. Bracketed in red, he wrote, "I suffer slightly in my left leg from the same cause I complained of at home, the San Jacinto wound."

7. A Fragile Republic

A large crowd gathered on the dock in New Orleans to meet the hero of San Jacinto. A young student from Alabama, Margaret Moffette Lea, would always remember that day. Once he was in the hospital, doctors removed the bone fragments from Houston's ankle, and he recovered quickly. He rested for a few weeks but returned to Texas.

David Burnett, the interim president of the Republic of Texas, called for an election to be held on September 5 to vote on the constitution and to elect government officials. Texans saw annexation of the independent nation to the United States as a possibility. The election also asked Texans for their opinion about annexation. Sam Houston did not seek the nomination for president of Texas, but with popular support, he changed his mind. He

This is the seal of the Republic of Texas that was taken from a sketch by Peter Craig (see page 62).

easily defeated Henry Smith and Stephen F. Austin. Texans unanimously approved the constitution and overwhelmingly supported annexation to the United States.

On October 22, 1836, Sam Houston became the first president of the Republic of Texas. Houston knew that Texas's future still was not secure. Many in the Texan army wanted revenge for Mexico's actions in Texas. To prevent an invasion of Mexico, Houston sent most of the Texan army home. Houston then sought recognition by the United States, but President Jackson feared Mexico's reaction. Jackson also did not want to upset the balance between slave states and free states in the United States. Those states opposed to slavery did not want to annex Texas, where slavery already existed.

The second problem was Santa Anna. The Texan congress held Santa Anna captive. Many Texans, remembering Santa Anna's cruelty, demanded he be executed. Sam Houston knew that executing Santa Anna might bring a harsh response from other nations. Houston, to improve Texas's chances of being recognized by the United States, wisely decided to release Santa Anna to Mexico. Santa Anna would return by way of Washington, D.C., where he would meet with President Jackson.

Santa Anna traveled to Washington, D.C., along with representatives of the Republic of Texas. Before he left, Santa Anna had agreed that once back in Mexico, he would work for Texas's recognition as an independent republic. Santa Anna spent several days meeting with

Jackson and others about the possibility of Mexico receiving payment for Texas. No agreement was made, and he left for Veracruz. Back in Mexico, he rejected his promise to work for recognition of Texan independence.

Texan representatives in Washington urged Congress to provide funds for a diplomatic agent for the Republic of Texas. On March 3, 1837, one day before Jackson left office, he recognized Texas as an independent nation and appointed a diplomatic representative.

In April 1837, Houston moved the capital of Texas from Columbia to Houston, the new town on Buffalo Bayou. There he worked to secure Texas's future.

Peter Krag presented this color sketch as the design
for the flag and seal of the Republic of Texas.
It was approved on Jauary 25, 1839.

That same month, Houston acted on his petition for divorce from Eliza Allen. In San Augustine, where the petition was filed, the court declared Houston divorced in a brief proceeding. Houston was now free to marry.

Houston appointed representatives to England and France to obtain trade agreements and financial assistance. England, fearing Mexico's reaction, did not take any action. The French were friendly, but they would not establish permanent relations at that time.

Houston submitted to the Texas Congress the treaty negotiated with the Cherokee in the winter of 1836. Congress, with the encouragement of Texas's vice president Mirabeau B. Lamar, refused to ratify it. New negotiations failed when a group of Mexicans and Indians in eastern Texas refused allegiance to the Republic of Texas. Houston sent a militia force, which defeated the rebels in October 1837. Houston pardoned all Indians for any part in the rebellion, but hope for a treaty was lost.

Under the Texas Constitution, a president could not serve two consecutive terms; consequently, Houston could not be reelected. Texas had no political parties, only those that supported Houston's policies, and those that opposed Houston's policies. With no strong candidate that agreed with Sam Houston, the opposition elected Mirabeau B. Lamar as president.

In 1839, Houston was invited to attend a festival at the plantation of William Bledsoe near Mobile, Alabama.

Mirabeau B. Lamar was born in Georgia on August 16, 1798.
As a boy, Lamar became a skilled horseman and fencer and began to
write poetry and paint. He first traveled to Texas in 1835, and decided
to move there. He was elected vice president of the Texas Republic in
1836, and was inaugurated as president in 1838. He died in 1859.

Sam Houston, the hero of San Jacinto attracted everyone's attention. When Sam Houston met Margaret Moffette Lea at the festival, he felt a special bond. Houston spent the next few days trying to win her heart. Margaret told him that since that day in May 1836, on the dock in New Orleans, she had thought of him often. Before Sam Houston left, he had Margaret's promise to marry him.

Houston returned to Nacogdoches in late September 1839. His

Margaret Moffette Lea married Sam Houston in 1840. This daguerreotype was taken in Galveston shortly after the marriage.

friends in San Augustine elected him in 1839 and in 1840, to serve two terms representing their district in the Texas Congress.

Following Page: This 1859 map of Texas was created by A. M. Gentry and shows the Sabine and Galveston Bay railroads that exist, that are under construction, or that have been planned but not yet contracted. Houston is highlighted in red. Austin, which was made the capital of Texas by Lamar, is highlighted in blue.

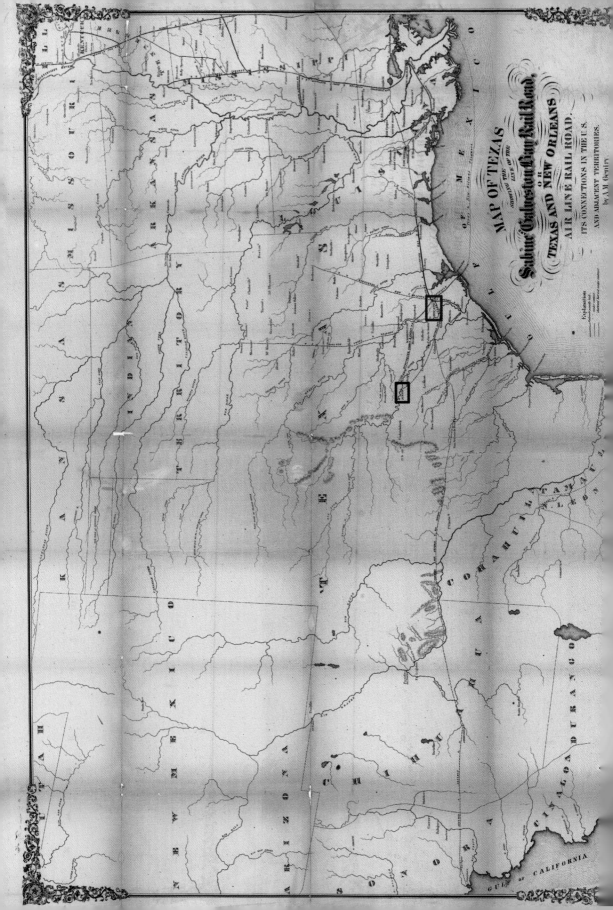

MAP OF TEXAS,
SHOWING THE LINE OF THE
Sabine, Galveston Bay Rail Road,
OR
TEXAS AND NEW ORLEANS
AIR LINE RAIL ROAD.
ITS CONNECTIONS IN THE U.S.
AND ADJACENT TERRITORIES.
By A. M. Gentry.

Explanation

President Lamar wasted no time in reversing many of Houston's policies. Lamar was pleased when, with his influence, Congress voted to move the capital from Houston to the small town of Waterloo on the frontier and to change its name to honor the "Father of Texas," Austin.

During this time, the Texas navy added to the tension between Texas and Mexico. The navy had become involved in a conflict between the Mexican government and the rebel forces in Yucatán. In the fall of 1841, Yucatán agreed to pay Texas $8,000 per month if the navy would help fight the Mexican government.

Despite their disagreement on many issues, Sam Houston applauded Mirabeau Lamar's success in establishing foreign relations. Countries such as France, England, and Holland recognized the Republic of Texas. These countries signed commercial treaties with Texas.

On May 9, 1840, Sam Houston and Margaret were married at her home in Marion, Alabama. She was 21 and he was 47. The

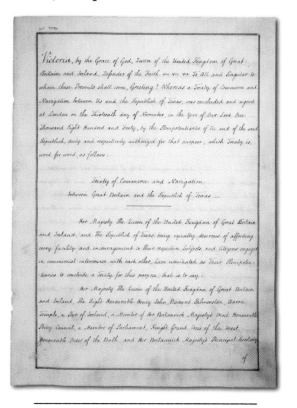

This treaty was signed on November 14, 1840, between Great Britain and the Republic of Texas. It was not put into effect until July 28, 1842.

newlyweds returned to Texas and settled in Houston.

Sam Houston and David Burnet were candidates for president of Texas in September 1841. Houston won by five thousand votes. The people again showed their confidence in Houston's leadership.

In December, Houston quickly went to work on the main problems in Texas: Indian policy, finances, and Mexico. He negotiated peace treaties and trade agreements with the Indians, which practically ended all the conflicts. Houston also made cuts in the republic's expenses, which almost balanced the budget.

Avoiding trouble with Mexico proved more difficult. Houston recalled the Texas navy ending its involvement in Mexico's problems. Lamar had proposed an unpopular expedition to Santa Fe to establish control there. The Santa Fe Expedition ended in disaster. Mexican troops forced the exhausted Texans to surrender without a shot being fired. The Texans were marched to Mexico City, where they were held in prison until 1842.

Mexico responded to the expedition by invading Texas twice in 1842. In the second invasion, the Texans defeated the Mexicans but allowed them to retreat to Mexico. Under pressure from the Texas Congress, Houston ordered the militia to pursue the Mexicans and if they saw a "prospect of success," to invade Mexico. When the Texans reached the Rio Grande, they found that the Mexicans had crossed into Mexico. Commander Alexander Somervell decided an invasion was not needed and ordered a retreat. About three hundred angry Texans refused the orders.

The remaining Texans crossed the river and entered the town of Mier demanding supplies and money. When Mexican soldiers arrived at Mier, the eager Texans, not knowing the number of Mexican soldiers present, decided to attack. The Mexicans overwhelmed the outnumbered Texans. The Texans surrendered and were marched to Mexico City. On the way there the Texans escaped but were recaptured. Santa Anna ordered one of every ten Texans shot. The survivors joined their fellow Texans from the Santa Fe Expedition in prison.

Houston had opposed locating the capital in Austin. Based on the

The Missouri Compromise refers to legislative measures enacted by the U.S. Congress in 1820, which regulated the extension of slavery in the United States. When slaveholding Missourians applied for statehood in 1818, the long-standing balance of free and slave states (11 each) was jeopardized. Maine, then a part of Massachusetts, also applied for statehood in 1819. To compromise, Missouri was admitted as a slave state and Maine as a free state. Legislation passed prohibiting slavery from Louisiana Purchase territories north of 36° 30'.

trouble with Mexico, he wanted to move the government to Houston. The people of Austin resisted moving the archives, so Houston and Congress met at Washington-on-the-Brazos, a safer location. While there, Sam and Margaret Houston celebrated the birth of their first child, Sam Jr., on May 25, 1843.

Sam Houston appealed to the governments of Great Britain and the United States, as well as to the governments of other nations, to help end the crisis. In June 1843, Houston signed an armistice, which called for an end to the fighting, but neither side could agree to the terms. Mexico released a few prisoners at a time, and in September 1844, the remaining Texans were released.

On April 12, 1844, Secretary of State John C. Calhoun signed a treaty for Texas to become a territory of the United States. Annexation failed when it became an issue in the presidential campaign.

John C. Calhoun, shown here in a portrait by Archibald L. Dick, lived from 1782 to 1850, and served in the federal government from 1811 until his death.

Westward expansion dominated the presidential campaign of 1844. Northerners, free-soilers, and abolitionists viewed Texas's annexation as an attempt to expand slavery and to gain political power. Southerners feared

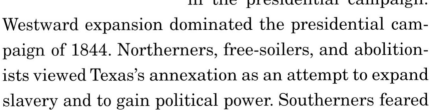

that the efforts to prevent annexation of another slave state were attempts to weaken their economy and political strength. Also, Mexico refused to recognize Texas as an independent republic. Many American citizens feared Mexico's reaction if attempts to annex Texas resumed. The nomination and election of James K. Polk as U.S. president, on an expansionist platform, ensured that the issue of annexation would be raised in U.S. Congress.

James K. Polk, here in an 1846 painting by George Peter Alexander Healy, was the eleventh U.S. president. He served from 1845 to 1849.

As before, Houston could not run for president in the next election. Secretary of State Anson Jones, who agreed with Houston's policies, won an easy victory.

Houston knew that annexation was not a certainty. Always fearful of another conflict with Mexico, Houston worked to maintain foreign relations with other nations. Houston maintained Texas's security and continued trade and investments until the political tide in the United States turned toward annexation.

Before he left office, President Tyler sought annexation through a joint resolution of Congress requiring a simple majority rather than by a treaty requiring two-thirds approval. On February 27, 1845, the House approved the joint resolution. The Senate passed an amended version, which the House of Representatives approved. Under joint resolution, Texas retained all its public lands to sell to pay off debts, and the Missouri

Andrew Jackson is shown here in a portrait taken between 1844 and 1845, by Edward Anthony, a photographer in Mathew Brady's studio. Jackson is leaning against a pillow, which gives evidence of his illness during the last year of his life.

Compromise line, dividing slave and free territory, was extended through Texas's northern boundary.

Sam, Margaret, and Sam Jr. planned a trip to visit relatives in Alabama and then Andrew Jackson in Nashville. In New Orleans, they heard that Jackson was dying. They rushed to Nashville but arrived too late. On June 8, 1845, Houston lost his friend and the most important political influence in his life. Houston called his young son to his side and told him to "remember that you have looked on the face of Andrew Jackson."

On July 4, a special session of the Texas Congress approved the terms of annexation. That fall Texans voted overwhelmingly to support it. On December 29, 1845, Texas entered the Union as the twenty-eighth state.

A large crowd gathered at the capitol in Austin, Texas, on February 19, 1846. President Anson Jones ended his speech by declaring, "The final act of this great drama is now performed. The Republic of Texas is no More." As the Lone Star flag was lowered, Houston stepped forward and caught the flag in his arms.

Thomas J. Rusk represented Texas, along with Houston, in the U.S. Senate from 1854 to 1857.

Two days later the Texas legislature selected Sam Houston and Thomas J. Rusk to represent Texas in the U.S. Senate. On March 30, Houston took the seat he would occupy for the next thirteen years.

Sam, Margaret, and Sam Jr. were living on their plantation, Raven Hill, east of Huntsville, Texas. In September 1846, the Houstons celebrated the birth of a daughter, Nancy Elizabeth. The following spring, while Houston was in Washington, D.C., Margaret had successful, but at the time life-threatening, surgery to remove a breast tumor. Houston knew his duties would keep him away from home a great deal. To ensure his family's comfort and for his peace of mind, Houston decided to look for another place to live.

8. Senator Houston

President Polk, in his first message to Congress in 1845, called for an end to the joint U.S. and British occupation of the Oregon Country. That same year John L. O'Sullivan coined the term Manifest Destiny. In an editorial supporting Polk's expansion policy, he wrote that it was the United States's "manifest destiny to overspread and to possess the whole continent."

The British rejected Polk's offer to settle the Oregon boundary at the forty-ninth parallel. As negotiations continued, in the spring of 1846, the Senate debated terminating the joint occupation treaty with Great Britain.

Sam Houston addressed the Senate, supporting President Polk. Houston recognized the importance of the popular vote and also that the election had granted Polk public support to resolve the Oregon issue. In April, the Senate and the House passed a resolution to terminate joint occupation of Oregon. Polk notified the British, as required by the treaty. In June 1846, the United States and Britain established the forty-ninth parallel as the boundary between the United States and Canada.

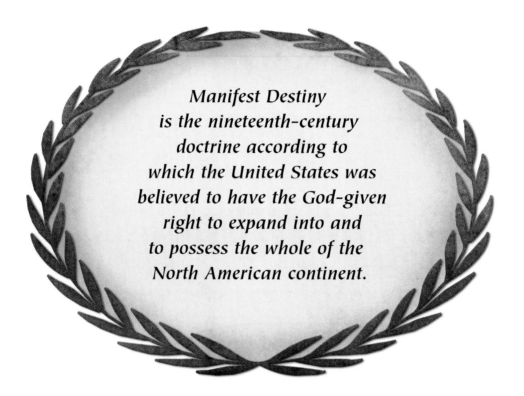

*Manifest Destiny
is the nineteenth-century
doctrine according to
which the United States was
believed to have the God-given
right to expand into and
to possess the whole of the
North American continent.*

The U.S. troops sent to Texas during the annexation process were still stationed on the border between Texas and Mexico. On May 11, 1846, the government heard that Mexican soldiers had attacked U.S. troops on April 25. President Polk informed congress: "Mexico has . . . invaded our territory and shed American blood upon the American soil." Two days later Polk signed a declaration of war.

After many U.S. victories, on September 12, 1847, U.S. troops captured the hill of Chapultepec and the gates into Mexico City. Two days later troops raised the U.S. flag over the National Palace. On September 16, President

The Oregon Country is outlined in blue on this detail from an 1846 map of Texas, Oregon, and California created by Samuel Augustus Mitchell. Polk used the idea of Manifest Destiny in his argument to make Oregon a U.S. state.

Santa Anna resigned, and the Mexican government informed the United States it wanted to negotiate peace.

The United States and Mexico signed the Treaty of Guadalupe Hidalgo in early 1848. Mexico recognized Texas's annexation and the Rio Grande as the border. Mexico received $15 million, and the United States assumed debts owed to the United States by Mexico. They acquired Mexico's territory including all or parts of the present states of California, Nevada, Utah, Colorado, New Mexico, Oklahoma, Kansas, Wyoming, and Arizona.

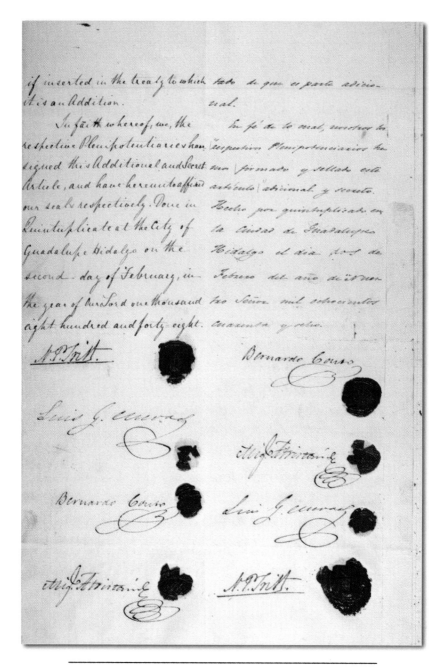

The Treaty of Guadalupe Hidalgo ended the Mexican-American War and added 1,193,061 square miles (3,090,014 sq km) of land to the United States's territory, including the territory of Texas above the Rio Grande, New Mexico, and California.

Continued westward expansion raised the old issue of the extension of slavery. The Missouri Compromise of 1820 had resolved the problem for the area acquired in the Louisiana Purchase. It prohibited slavery north of the southern boundary of Missouri. The compromise, however, did not settle the question for future expansion.

Around this time, the Houstons moved into their new house, Woodland Home, in Huntsville, Texas. In April their third child, Margaret Lea, was born.

In 1848, the U.S. Senate began debating the establishment of a territorial government for Oregon. Most members of Congress, including Houston, felt that slavery as

Houston designed the home that his family occupied in 1848, in Huntsville, and that they lived in periodically until it was sold in 1858. He referred to it as "our dear Woodland Home." In a letter from the summer of 1851, he wrote about his life there, saying that he was "farming in a small way . . . and busy as a bee in a tar barrel."

an economic system would never be extended to Oregon. John C. Calhoun argued that settlers should be able to take slaves into Oregon. Houston accused Calhoun of "little agitations" that were not in the best interest of the Union. The Missouri Compromise applied to Oregon.

Sam Houston supported the Oregon Bill, which passed in the House and the Senate in 1848, establishing the territorial government and prohibiting slavery. He believed the Missouri Compromise was as binding as the Constitution. Calhoun blamed the loss in part on Houston's siding with the North and supporting the bill.

At a meeting of southerners in Congress early in 1849, legislators signed the Southern Address, written by John C. Calhoun. The Address condemned the "systematic agitation" against slavery. It called actions by the North "acts of aggression against the South."

In the Senate, Sam Houston answered Calhoun. Houston criticized Calhoun because he urged "revolutionary convulsions" and encouraged "sectional jealousy and disunion." Houston pledged, "I would lay down my life to defend any one of the States from aggression." More important, he said he would defend the Union because "the destruction of the Union would be the ruin of all States." He viewed the "course pursued by Mr. Calhoun, and the Abolitionists tend to the same end" because they both threatened to destroy the Union.

General Zachary Taylor won the presidential election of 1848. After the 1849 gold rush, President Taylor proposed that California be admitted as a state and be allowed to decide on slavery for itself. His proposal shocked the South. Slaveholders had not taken their property to California, so everyone understood California would enter the union as a free state. The admission of California as a free state would upset the balance of power between slave and free states.

On February 8, Sam Houston repeated his conviction that Congress had no power to legislate on slavery in the territories and states. By maintaining the Missouri Compromise, it "let the north abstain from all encroachments upon Southern rights." He said, "We do not ask the North to concede anything. We merely ask them to abstain from aggression."

Houston wanted past differences resolved. In closing, Houston said, "For a nation divided against itself cannot stand. I wish, if this Union must be dissolved, that its ruins may be the monument of my grave, and the graves of my family. I wish no epitaph to be written to tell that I survive the ruin of this glorious Union."

In July 1850, Vice President Millard Fillmore became president. Fillmore broke the deadlock between Congress and the White House. By the end of 1850, the House and

Following Spread: Edwin Ferry Johnson created this map of the United States and Mexico in 1853. The boundaries of all the states were not as they are today, but the United States was in possession of much of the land that would make them up. The California border is highlighted in blue.

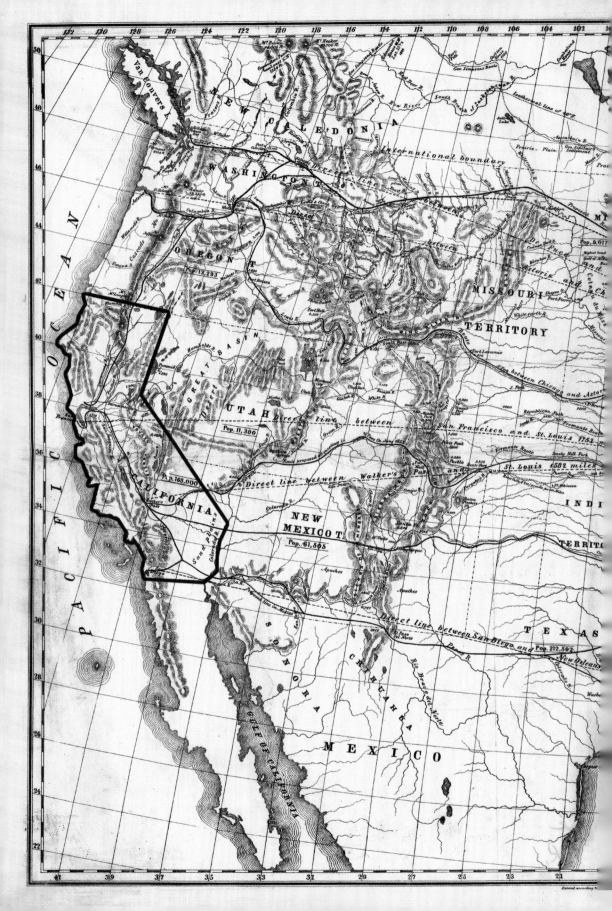

Map
OF THE
Proposed NORTHER...
Railroad ...
PACI...

by Edwin F. Jo...
1853.

Scale in Statute...

Senate had approved the compromise resolutions, known as the Compromise of 1850, introduced by Henry Clay. California entered the Union as the thirty-first state. The new state prohibited slavery. The territories of New Mexico and Utah were created to enter the Union when ready, with or without slavery depending on their constitutions. Texas's boundary was adjusted, and in exchange for the territory, the U.S. government paid off $10 million of Texas's debt. The Fugitive Slave Act was amended to benefit slave owners. A final resolution outlawed the slave trade, but not slavery, in the District of Columbia.

Sam Houston was one of only two southern senators who voted for all provisions. His commitment to preserve the Union in this crisis proved his willingness to place his convictions above all else.

The Compromise of 1850 calmed the divisions in the country. Even though most people did not agree with all the resolutions, they felt that because everyone had benefited, it was a fair solution to the crisis. No one knew that the Compromise of 1850 would only last four years.

Over the next four years, the Houston family grew. Mary William was born on April 9, 1850, and Antoinette Power was born on January 20, 1852. Both were born in the Woodland Home. On June 21, 1854, Sam Jr. finally got the little brother he hoped for with the birth of Andrew Jackson Houston at Independence, Texas.

9. Standing Alone

In 1854, Senator Stephen Douglas of Illinois introduced legislation, with no mention of slavery, to organize the Nebraska territory west of Iowa and Missouri. This would help in building a transcontinental railroad. The South supported a transcontinental railroad, but wanted a southern route. Nebraska lay above the Missouri Compromise line. Realizing the federal government would support only one project, competition arose between the northern industrial states and the agricultural states of the South.

To gain the support of southern Democrats, Douglas proposed the Kansas-Nebraska Act. In it, he agreed to divide the Nebraska Territory into Kansas and Nebraska. He included provisions repealing the Missouri Compromise and allowing the territories to make their own decisions based on popular sovereignty. Rumors spread in the North that the West would be opened to slavery.

On February 14, Sam Houston addressed the Senate, opposing the Kansas-Nebraska Act. Indians

SPEECH

OF

SENATOR HOUSTON, OF TEXAS,

ON THE NEBRASKA AND KANSAS BILL,

PREVIOUS TO THE FINAL PASSAGE OF THE SAME BY THE SENATE OF THE UNITED STATES,

FRIDAY NIGHT, MARCH 3, 1854.

The Senate having under consideration the bill to organize the Territories of Nebraska and Kansas—

Mr. HOUSTON said: Mr. President, this unusual night sitting is without precedent in the history of any previous Congress at this stage of the session. The extraordinary circumstances in which we find ourselves placed would seem to indicate a crisis in the affairs of the country of no ordinary importance; a crisis that portends either good or evil to our institutions.

The extraordinary character of the bill before the Senate, as well as the manner in which it is presented to the body, demands the gravest deliberation. This, sir, is the anniversary of a protracted session, in which the organization of the Territory of Nebraska was elaborately discussed on the last day of the last session. In that discussion which, like this, had kept us in our seats to the morning dawn, the prominent points of opposition were such as related to the Indian tribes. Such a bill at the present session would have met with no insuperable objections; but what do we now find? A bill entirely variant, and a bill which involves new and important principles. It has come an unexpected measure without a harbinger, for no agitation was heard of, and the breeze bore no whisper to our ears that the Missouri compromise was to be repealed.

Its presentation has been as sudden as the measure itself is bold; and the excitement of the public mind is of corresponding intensity. We are told, to be sure, that there is no necessity for agitation, and that soon the public mind will be tranquil, and the country will be in a state of repose and quiet—as it was at the introduction of this measure. The honorable Senator who has just taken his seat, [Mr. DOUGLAS,] the chairman of the Committee on Territories, in his lecture to the South, exhorted them to stand by the principle of this bill, with the assurance that it will be good for them, and that the country will maintain it. Sir, under proper circumstances, I should recognize the exhortation; but is the principle such a one as should be adopted by this body, or can it be sanctioned by the nation? Whether it is expedient and useful at this time I shall take the liberty to examine.

Mr. President, I cannot believe that the agitation created by this measure will be confined to the Senate Chamber. I cannot believe, from what we have witnessed here to-night, that this will be the exclusive arena for the exercise of human passions, and the expression of public opinions. If the Republic be not shaken I will thank Heaven for its kindness in maintaining its stability. To what extent is it proposed to establish the principle of non-intervention? Are you extending it to a domain inhabited by citizens, or to a barren prairie, a wilderness, or even to forty thousand wild Indians? Is this the diffusive excellence of non-intervention? I, sir, am for non-intervention upon the principles which have heretofore been recognized by this Government. Hitherto Territories have been organized—within my recollection Alabama, Missouri, Florida, Arkansas, Mississippi, Wisconsin, and Iowa have been organized—and the principle now proposed was not deemed essential to their well-being; and is there any infirmity in their constitutions or their growth? Sir, has any malign influence attached to them from their simple, economical organization? It may be that the word "economy" is deemed obsolete in the present condition of our Treasury. Were it otherwise, I am simple enough to confess that the organization of two Territories—when there are not people to constitute an ordinary county in one of the populous States of this Union, and when those who do inhabit the Territories are United States soldiers, who are not entitled to vote at elections in the States or Territories—is not a procedure that can be characterized as economical. If the principle of non-intervention be correct, it is correct where the Territories have been governed by laws of Congress until they are prepared to make application for admission as States. Then they have a right to elect their delegates to convention, for the purpose of framing State constitutions, which, if accepted by Congress, invest them with all the sovereign rights of States; and then, for the first time, they have the complete power of

Houston spoke passionately in opposition of the Kansas-Nebraska Bill. Here is the first page of the speech he made to the Senate on Friday, March 3, 1854. He feels sure this bill will be the downfall of the Union. He says, "If the Republic be not shaken I will thank Heaven for its kindness in maintaining its stability."

held or occupied all of Kansas. Houston appealed to the government to honor its commitments. They had relocated Indians to the area with assurances that they would not be disturbed. The act violated "a pledge, most solemnly given." Now, "it seems to be a foregone conclusion that the Indians must yield to the progress of the white man. They must go from place to place, and that there is to be no rest for them." Finally he pleaded, "They are human beings. Protect them Senators, guard them."

The next day Houston continued his remarks, turning to the repeal of the Missouri Compromise. He reminded the Senate that the compromise had been "recognized and acted upon by Congress as a solemn compact between States." He viewed it as "essential to the preservation of this Union, and to the very existence of the South." Repeal the compromise and "you are putting the knife to the throat of the South." He predicted that without the compromise "at some future day the South will be overwhelmed."

On March 3, Houston again addressed the Senate. In his speech, he pleaded, "Upon the decision which we make upon this question, must depend union or disunion. Maintain the Missouri compromise! Stir not up agitation! Give us peace!"

On May 22, the House passed the Kansas-Nebraska Act and two days later the Senate approved it. Sam Houston stood alone as the only southern Senator to

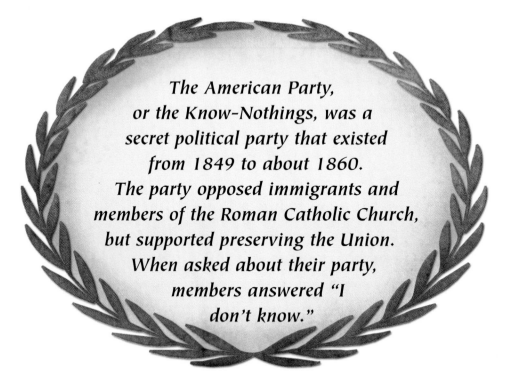

The American Party,
or the Know-Nothings, was a
secret political party that existed
from 1849 to about 1860.
The party opposed immigrants and
members of the Roman Catholic Church,
but supported preserving the Union.
When asked about their party,
members answered "I
don't know."

oppose the act. Newspapers and politicians branded Sam Houston as a traitor to the South. Houston answered, "while it was the most unpopular vote" he ever cast, "it was the wisest and most patriotic." He predicted a grave outcome. "I see my beloved South go down in the unequal contest, in a sea of blood and smoking ruin."

In November 1855, at a barbecue for the American Party, or the Know-Nothings, Houston answered the charges of favoring the North. He was a southerner but all his "sacred ties could never render [him] unfaithful to the Union." Houston declared: "I will say there are but two planks in the platform on which I stand—the

Constitution and the Union." He said, "by one I am guided, with the other I am willing to perish."

Houston realized that with the rumors of his sympathy for the North, he would not be reelected as a senator. Houston had other plans. In 1857, he decided to run for governor of Texas.

Houston traveled across the state in an exhausting campaign. In one community, the people, still angry over his votes in the Senate, refused to let him speak in the courthouse. Houston agreed he did not live or pay taxes in their community. Instead, he invited anyone that wished to hear him to follow him to the large oak tree on a hillside "on the soil of Texas. I have a right to speak there because I watered it with my blood."

Texans supported southern issues and feared northern extremists. They did not trust Sam Houston to fight for their beliefs. Hardin Runnels won the election by more than four thousand votes, the only man to ever defeat Sam Houston in a political contest.

That same year, 1857, the U.S. Supreme Court found the Missouri Compromise unconstitutional in the Dred Scott decision. Northerners feared the South would demand the extension of slavery into free states. Southerners felt the abolitionists must be stopped.

William Rogers Houston, the Houstons' third son, was born in May 1858, at Huntsville. Later that year, Houston sold the Woodland Home and its surrounding property to help pay off expenses from his campaign for governor.

Sam Houston returned to the U.S. Senate to complete his term. On March 4, 1859, he ended his career in the Senate. The Washington *Evening Star* reported: "This distinguished man left Washington yesterday afternoon for his home in Texas. Up to the hour of his departure, his rooms were crowded by his friends calling to take leave of him. No other public man ever made more, or more sincere friends here."

William Rogers Houston was the third son born to Sam and Margaret Houston. He was not a strong child and his mother worried for him, but he grew to be strong. As an adult, he became a special officer of the Indian Service.

At the end of his term, Sam Houston stood alone in the South, unwilling to abandon his convictions. Houston carried his hope of maintaining the Union home to Texas.

10. "Blood and Smoking Ruin"

Sam Houston once again entered the race for governor of Texas in 1859. This time he made only one speech, and he defeated Runnels by almost the same margin by which he had been beaten two years before.

On December 21, 1859, Houston made his inaugural address. He stressed that Texas had "entered not into the North, nor into the South, but into the Union." Texas, like the other states, had different interests but relied "upon the same Constitution as they to secure her in the enjoyment of her rights." Houston urged Texas to make the "Constitution the guiding star of our career as a State."

In January 1860, Houston received the Resolutions from

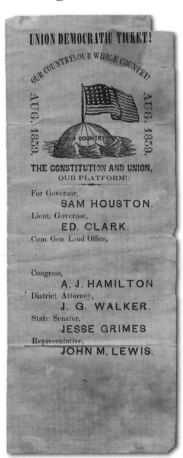

This is the Union Democratic Ticket from August 1859.

South Carolina asserting the rights of the South. It included the right of a state to secede. Houston delivered the Resolutions to the legislature with a personal message. He condemned the extremists in the North and South, warning, "whenever we cease" to respect the Constitution, "as the only means of securing free government, no hope remains for the advocates of regulated liberty." In Houston's view "there will be no Union to secede from, for in the death of the Constitution, the Union likewise perishes; and then comes civil war." Houston recommended adopting the Resolutions without the provision on secession.

Having his family with him was a great comfort during those difficult days. The Houston's fourth son, Temple Lea, was born on August 12, 1860, the first child born in the Governor's Mansion in Austin. Supporters raised the possibility of a "Houston for President" campaign. Houston had friends and political ties in all areas of the country. He seriously considered the possibility and certainly would have accepted the nomination. However, when he realized his name might cause further divisions in the country, Houston withdrew as a serious candidate.

Political parties met in 1860, to select candidates for the presidential election in November. Democrats, unable to agree on a candidate, disbanded their convention. Southern Democrats, supporting slavery, chose John C. Breckinridge. Northern Democrats selected Stephen

Douglas, on a platform of popular sovereignty. A coalition of Democrats, Whigs, and former Know-Nothings formed the Constitutional Union Party, which support-ed the Constitution and opposed sectional-ism. They nominated John Bell. Republicans met in Chicago and on the third ballot select-ed Abraham Lincoln on a free-soil platform.

Sam Houston spoke to the men gathered at a meeting of the Constitutional Union Party in September 1860. Houston urged the people to judge each candidate up for election "on the princi-ples they announce." As for Lincoln, the Republican candidate, Houston recommend-ed, "The Union is worth more than Mr. Lincoln, and if the battle is to be fought for the Constitution, let us fight it in the Union and for the sake of the

Abraham Lincoln, shown here in an 1887 portrait by George Peter Alexander Healy, lived from 1809 to 1865. He served from 1861 to 1865 as the sixteenth president of the United States. He served in this role during the Civil War, though he died before the war ended.

Union." If elected, and Lincoln "administers the Government in accordance with the Constitution, our rights must be respected. If he does not, the Constitution has provided a remedy. Let the people say to these abolition agitators of the North, and to the disunion agitators of the South, You cannot dissolve this Union."

The move for secession intensified when news of Lincoln's victory reached Texas. On December 20, 1860, South Carolina seceded, increasing demands for secession in Texas. Houston advised the legislature to listen to the people "as the source of all power," for they "can alone declare the course that Texas shall pursue." He suggested that if secession passed, Texas should remain independent, "unfurling once again her Lone Star Banner."

On January 29, 1861, the secession convention passed a resolution for Texas to secede. On February 1, they approved it. On February 23, the voters overwhelmingly supported secession.

Houston's only hope was for Texas to remain independent. He questioned the convention's authority to join the Confederacy without a popular vote. To silence Houston, the convention decided to require all state officials to take a loyalty oath to the Confederacy.

On the night of March 15, Houston went to his bedroom upstairs in the Governor's Mansion. All night he paced the floor and wrestled with his decision. The next morning, Sam told Margaret "I will never do it." He would not sacrifice his principles and take the oath of allegiance to the Confederacy.

The next day, Houston quietly sat whittling in the basement of the capitol as his name was called, three times. He refused to answer. The legislature declared the governor's office vacant and appointed a successor.

Houston sat alone in his office writing his final message to the people of Texas. "I love Texas too well to bring civil strife and bloodshed upon her. I am stricken down now, because I will not yield those principles, which I have fought for and struggled to maintain. The severest pang is the blow comes in the name of the State of Texas."

On April 12, 1861, Confederate guns fired on the Union forces at Fort Sumter in Charleston Harbor. The fort surrendered after a day and night of continuous shelling. The civil war that Houston feared had begun. Houston wondered whether Texas and the South would suffer the "blood and smoking ruin" he had predicted.

In the fall of 1862, the Houstons moved back to Huntsville. Houston could not repurchase the Woodland Home, so they rented the Steamboat House from Rufus Bailey, president of Austin College. The house got its name because of its unusual design, which resembled a paddleboat on the Mississippi River.

That spring Houston's health declined. The shoulder wound from Horseshoe Bend was especially troubling. In April, Houston drew up his will, leaving his property and the care of the children to Margaret. He left his sword

In pursuance of the sixth section of the act of Congress entitled "An act to suppress insurrection and to punish treason and rebellion, to seize and confiscate property of rebels, and for other purposes" Approved July 17. 1862, and which act, and the Joint Resolution explanatory thereof, are herewith published, I, Abraham Lincoln, President of the United States, do hereby proclaim to, and warn all persons within the contemplation of said sixth section to cease participating in, aiding, countenancing, or abetting the existing rebellion, or any rebellion against the government of the United States, and to return to their proper allegiance to the United States, on pain of the forfeitures and seizures, as within and by said sixth section provided—

And I hereby make known that it is my purpose, upon the next meeting of Congress, to again recommend the adoption of a practical measure for tendering pecuniary aid to the free choice or rejection, of any and all States, which may then be recognizing and practically sustaining the authority of the United States, and which may then have voluntarily adopted, or thereafter may voluntarily adopt, gradual abolishment of slavery within such State or States— that the object is to practically restore, thenceforward to maintain, the constitutional relation between the general government, and each, and all the States, wherein that relation

Above is the first page of the Emancipation Proclamation, which would go into effect on January 1, 1863. Even though this document had no real power in 1863, it has become one of the most important documents in American history. It set the stage for enslaved blacks to gain freedom and equal rights.

from the Battle of San Jacinto to Sam Jr. with the request it "be drawn only in defense of the Constitution, the Laws, and Liberties of his Country."

When word of Lincoln's Emancipation Proclamation reached Texas, Houston called Joshua, Eliza, Jeff, and the other slaves to the porch of the Steamboat House. He read the words from the newspaper and explained what freedom would mean to them. The proclamation issued by Abraham Lincoln would take effect on January 1, 1863.

In June, Houston traveled to Sour Lake to rest and to regain his strength. After a month, he returned to Huntsville feeling a bit better. Houston enjoyed his days in Huntsville and being with his family. He would walk to town and sit whittling in front of the Gibbs Store. The children loved his stories. Houston also enjoyed visiting with the Union soldiers who were being held at the Texas Penitentiary a few blocks from Steamboat House.

One afternoon Houston returned home with a chill and a fever. Margaret put him to bed in the downstairs room. His health worsened, and he drifted in and out of sleep. On July 26, with Margaret by his side, Sam Houston died at 6:15 P.M. His last words were "Texas, Texas, Margaret." Margaret called the children around her as she removed the ring from Houston's finger. She showed them the inscription, HONOR.

11. Sam Houston's Legacy

History will always remember Sam Houston's command of the army of Texas during the Texas Revolution and at the Battle of San Jacinto. Sam Houston's legacy, however, cannot be limited to a brief period in time or to a single battle. The legacy someone leaves to future generations can best be found not in his or her actions but in the character of that person.

Sam Houston's commitment to his principles stands above his military and political achievements. Whether one agrees or disagrees with Houston's actions, no one doubts his sincerity and devotion to the Republic of Texas, the state of Texas, and Native Americans.

Finally, Sam Houston's greatest commitment, the preservation of the Union, established his enduring legacy. Sam Houston committed himself to the principle that no institution, no state, and certainly no individual should destroy the Union. In his commitment to this principle, he challenged future generations, in the same way, to stand on sound principles and to defend them at any cost. In the end, as Andrew Jackson predicted, "The world will take care of Houston's fame."

Sam Houston is pictured here in an 1840s painting attributed to George Catlin, which looks similar to a painting by Louis Antoine Collas. Houston, here in a Republic of Texas uniform, lived a colorful, interesting life, but also one of principle. He was not afraid to stand up for what he believed was right. Today the Sam Houston Memorial Museum in Huntsville, Texas, keeps the legacy of this American hero alive.

Timeline

1793	On March 2, Sam Houston is born.
1809	Sam runs away from home.
1810	Sam is adopted by Chief Oo-loo-te-ka.
1812	Sam opens a private school. In June, the War of 1812 begins.
1813	Houston enlists in the regular army.
1814	In March, Houston is wounded during the Battle of Horseshoe Bend.
	On December 24, the War of 1812 ends.
1815	On January 8, forces under Andrew Jackson win the Battle of New Orleans.
1818	Houston passes the bar and begins law practice in Lebanon, Tennessee.
1819	Houston becomes attorney general of Tennessee's Nashville district.
1823	Houston is elected to the U.S. House of Representatives.
1827	Houston is elected governor of Tennessee.

1829   On April 23, Houston departs for Indian Territory.

On October 21, Houston becomes a Cherokee citizen.

In December, Houston represents the Cherokee Nation in Washington, D.C.

1832   Houston is accused of fraud but is cleared.

Houston goes to Texas.

1833   On April 1, Houston attends the Second Convention in San Felipe, Texas.

1835   In November, the Consultation meets.

1836   On March 1, Houston attends the Texas Constitutional Convention.

In March, Texas declares its independence. Houston takes command of the army. The Alamo falls, and Houston retreats east.

On April 21, Houston's army wins the decisive Battle of San Jacinto.

On September 5, Houston is elected president of the Republic of Texas.

1841   On December 12, Houston begins his

second term as president of Texas.

1845 On December 29, Texas becomes the twenty-eighth state admitted to the Union.

1846 Mexican-American War begins.

1848 On January 24, Houston is sworn in for his first full term as a U.S. senator.

On February 2, the Treaty of Guadalupe Hidalgo is signed.

1859 In March, Houston leaves the U.S. Senate.

On December 21, Houston is inaugurated as governor of Texas.

1860 On December 20, South Carolina is the first state to secede from the Union.

1861 Texas Secession Convention passes resolution to secede, and the voters support it. Houston refuses to take the oath of allegiance to the Confederacy.

On April 12, the Civil War begins at Fort Sumter.

1862 On September 22, the Emancipation Proclamation is issued.

1863 On July 26, Houston dies of pneumonia in the Steamboat House at Huntsville.

Glossary

abolitionists (a-buh-LIH-shun-ists) People who worked to do away with slavery during the eighteenth and nineteenth centuries.

aggression (uh-GREH-shun) Threatening behavior or actions.

agitations (a-jih-TAY-shunz) Actions intended to excite public feelings.

ambassador (am-BA-suh-dor) Somebody who serves as an official representative.

annexation (a-nek-SAY-shun) The joining of a territory into another country, state, or other political entity.

apprentice (uh-PREN-tis) Somebody who works under a skilled professional in order to learn and become qualified in a trade.

armistice (AR-mis-tis) A truce or ceasefire in a war to discuss terms for peace.

breastworks (BREST-werks) An earthen wall built to chest height as a temporary barrier for defense.

commissioned (kuh-MIH-shund) An officer of the armed forces holding by a commission a rank of second lieutenant or ensign or above.

compromise (KOM-pruh-myz) The settlement of a dispute in which two or more sides agree to accept less than they originally wanted.

convulsions (kun-VUL-shunz) Extreme disruptions or disturbances.

customs (KUH-stumz) Taxes payable on imports and exports.

delegation (deh-luh-GAY-shun) A group of people chosen to represent or act on behalf of others.

depression (dih-PREH-shun) A state of unhappiness.

despair (dih-SPEHR) An intense feeling that there is no hope.

devastated (DEH-vuh-stayt-ed) A feeling of being overwhelmed or helpless.

encroachments (en-KROHCH-ments) Slowly taking away somebody's authority, rights, or property.

epitaph (EH-pih-taf) An inscription on a tombstone or monument commemorating a person.

fraud (FROD) The crime of obtaining money or some other benefit by intentional deception.

free-soil (FREE-soyl) A political view opposing the extension of slavery before the Civil War.

joint resolution (JOYNT reh-zuh-LOO-shun) A

resolution passed by both houses of a legislative
body that has the force of law when signed by or
passed over the veto of the executive branch.

legacy (LEH-guh-see) Something that is handed down
or remains from a previous generation or time.

militia (mi-LIH-shuh) An army of soldiers who are
civilians but take military training and can serve
full-time during emergencies.

negotiate (neh-GOH-shee-ayt) To work out terms or to
reach an agreement

parallel (PA-ruh-lel) One of the imaginary circles on
the surface of Earth paralleling the equator and
marking the latitude.

popular sovereignty (PAH-pyoo-lar SOV-ren-tee) A
political doctrine that the people of territories should
decide for themselves whether their territories would
enter the Union as free or slave states.

provisional government (pruh-VIH-zhun-ul GUH-
ver-ment) A temporary government established to
act before a permanent government.

quorum (KWO-rum) The number of people required to
be present to conduct business.

rations (RA-shuns) A fixed and limited amount of food,
supplied to somebody or to a group.

seceded (seh-SEED-ed) Formally withdrew from

membership in an organization, state, or alliance.

secession (suh-SEH-shun) A formal withdrawal from an organization, state, or alliance.

sectionalism (SEK-shnuh-lih-zum) Concern for the interests of a particular group rather than the whole.

titles (TY-tulz) Documents giving legal ownership.

transcontinental (trans-kon-tih-NEN-tul) Extending across a continent.

tribunal (try-BYOO-nul) A body that is appointed to make a judgment or inquiry.

tyranny (TEER-uh-nee) Cruelty and injustice in the exercising of power or authority over others.

unanimously (yoo-NA-nuh-mus-lee) Shared as a view by all, with nobody disagreeing.

wigwam (WIG-wom) A Native American building.

Additional Resources

To learn more about Sam Houston and the history of Texas, check out the following books and Web sites.

Books

Campbell, Randolph B. *Sam Houston and the American Southwest*. Boston: Addison-Wesley Publishing, 1993.

Fritz, Jean. *Make Way for Sam Houston*. New York: Putnam, 1986.

Web Sites

Due to the changing nature of Internet links, PowerPlus Books has developed an online list of Web sites related to the subject of this book. This site is updated regularly. Please use this link to access the list:

www.powerkidslinks.com/lalt/houston

Bibliography

Books

De Bruhl, Marshall. *Sword of San Jacinto, A Life of Sam Houston*. New York: Random House, Inc., 1993.

Friend, Llerena B. *Sam Houston, The Great Designer*. Austin: University of Texas Press, 1954.

James, Marquis. *The Raven, A Biography of Sam Houston*. New York: Blue Ribbon Books, 1936.

James, Marquis, and Bessie Rowland James. *Six Feet Six, The Heroic Story of Sam Houston*. Indianapolis, IN: The Bobbs-Merrill Company, 1931.

Roberts, Madge Thornall. *Star of Destiny, The Private Life Of Sam and Margaret Houston*. Denton, TX: University of North Texas Press, 1993.

Roberts, Madge Thornall, ed. *The Personal Correspondence of Sam Houston*. 4 Vols. Denton, TX: University of North Texas Press, 1996–2001.

Wade, Mary Dodson. *I Am Houston*. Houston: Colophon House, 1993.

Williams, Amelia W. and Eugene C. Barker, eds. *The Writings of Sam Houston*. 8 Vols. Austin: University of Texas Press, 1938–1943.

Index

About the Author

Walter M. Woodward, a sixth-generation Texan, is the curator of collections at the Sam Houston Memorial Museum in Huntsville, Texas. He is responsible for the care and preservation of the museum's historic buildings, including Sam Houston's Woodland Home and law office, and the Steamboat House. The museum also contains the largest collection of Sam Houston artifacts and the personal correspondence of Sam and Margaret Houston. Woodward received a B.A. in history from Sam Houston State University and an M.A. in history from the University of Houston.

Credits

Photo Credits

Cover: The R.W. Norton Art Gallery (portrait); Texas State Library and Archives Commission (painting); pp. 4, 24, 25, 59, 65, 79, 86, 90, 91 Sam Houston Memorial Museum, Huntsville, Texas; pp. 7, 14, 35, 66, 77, 82–83 Library of Congress Geography and Map Division Washington, D.C.; p. 9 © Prints George; pp. 11, 29, 53, 70 Library of Congress Prints and Photographs Division, Washington, D.C.; p. 17 National Museum of American Art, Washington, D.C./Art Resource, New York; p. 20 W. H. Coverdale Collection of Canadiana, National Archives of Canada, Ottowa; pp. 27, 78 © CORBIS; pp. 28, 45 San Jacinto Museum of History; p. 30 © North Carolina Museum of History; pp. 40, 42, 49, 56–57, 60, 62, 67 Texas State Library and Archives Commission; p. 47 © SuperStock; pp. 50–51 Map Collection, Center for American History, UT Austin; p. 51 (inset) Amon Carter Museum, Fort Worth, Texas, gift of Mrs. Anne Burnett Tandy in memory of her father Thomas Loyd Burnett, 1870–1938; p. 64 Mary and John Gray Library, Lamar University; pp. 71, 93 © the Corcoran Gallery of Art/CORBIS; p. 72 Daguerreotype Collection, Library of Congress Prints and Photographs Division, Washington, D.C.; p. 73 East Texas Research Center, Stephen F. Austin State University; p. 96 courtesy of the Robert Todd Lincoln Family Papers, Manuscript Division; p. 99 the R. W. Norton Art Gallery.

Editor Joanne Randolph
Series Design Laura Murawski
Layout Design Corinne Jacob
Photo Researcher Jeffrey Wendt